Battleborne Ben

Battleborne Ben

By

L.T. Hutchinson

Contents

Oh, The Places we Go!

"Ben-Ben, time for breakfast, sleepyhead," I heard my mom calling. Something sure smelled yummy.

Is Mom making bacon? *My favorite.* I opened my eyes and spotted moving boxes piled everywhere… hey, this wasn't my room…

I felt like someone punched me. Yesterday, we had moved into our new house on Fort Bragg, away from all my friends. Now I had to go to a new school – the third time in two years.

I pulled the pillow over my face. Nope. She can't bribe me to be happy about it, even with bacon.

"Don't forget to wash your face and brush your teeth before you come down," she called.

Rats. I fell out of my warm and comfy bed and stumbled into the bathroom, wishing I was back in Fort Hood with my buddies Chris and Fat Jimmy.

I dug through boxes until I found my favorite jeans and T-shirt, and my old high tops. "At least my clothes are the same," I grumbled to myself and dug some socks out of a suitcase.

"Ben! Get down here, please. Now."

I grabbed my old, gray sweatshirt and headed downstairs.

"Ouch!" I tripped on this really weird, twisty step and almost fell on my face. Stupid house.

I limped into the kitchen. "I hurt my foot on that stupid stair."

It didn't work. She ignored me.

"Morning, sweetheart." Mom put a plate of bacon and eggs, fresh strawberries, and toast in front of me and kissed the top of my head. "Ready for school?"

"No."

"No?"

"I want to go to my old school."

Mom sat down next to me and patted my hand. "I know it's hard for you to move again, Ben, but you know how Army life is. You and me, in this together."

"Why can't we be in this together in Fort Hood? I wanna play basketball with Chris and Fat Jimmy."

"I know you miss them, Ben. But trust me, you'll make new friends."

"But Fat Jimmy's dad said I could play basketball on his team this year. He said my hook shot was badass."

"Ben!"

"Sorry. But Mom…"

Mom stood. "Go get your backpack."

"My foot hurts."

Mom pulled back my chair.

"Can I have more orange juice?"

Mom's face did this thing where one eyebrow jumps up and her mouth gets all hard. That was her "no more nonsense" Look. I don't mess with that Look. I've seen big, strong soldiers take a step back when my mom, Captain Stark, shot them The Look.

"Okay, okay." I dragged my feet to the door and picked up my backpack.

Mom met me at the door. She made the shape of a heart and placed it over her heart, and I did the same and we both said together "We are a team." It was kinda corny, but it still made me feel better.

"Here's your lunch," Mom said, and tucked it into my backpack. "Let's go get you checked in. And honey?"

"What?"

"Try to have a good first day."

Yeah. Right.

Middle School Blues

This school looks like a prison, I thought as security guards made me walk through a sensor and put my backpack through an x-ray thingy.

I sat in the attendance office with my mom, getting checked in. Wasn't school supposed to be this cool place you go to exercise your brain and get smarter and stuff? This place had battle ship gray walls and floors and weird stains splattered on all of them.

And then there were the bars on all the windows. ALL the windows. Were they keeping bad people out? Or keeping us kids in?

The secretary handed me a schedule and my mom hugged me and left. I wandered the halls and finally came across the numbers 410. Oh boy. Homeroom.

I walked into the classroom and all eyes landed on me.

The teacher smiled at me. She looked okay – kinda pretty for a grown-up, with hair up in a bun, and glasses perched on the end of her nose.

"You must be Ben Stark," she said. "I'm Mrs. Gentry, but the kids call me Miss G." She held out her hand for my admission slip. I held it out, took a step, and bam! Hit the floor. Dangit! I tripped on my own big feet, which were having a hard time figuring out which foot goes first.

Kids bust out laughing and I closed my eyes and wished I was back in my old school.

"That will be quite enough," said Miss G, and the laughing stopped.

Miss G helped me up and pointed at an empty seat. I beelined for it, and almost made it when a big black boot jumped out and tripped me.

Wham! Aaaaand I'm on the floor. Again.

"Harry! Go see the principal immediately," Miss G said. "And I better hear an accurate report from him about what happened here."

Hands pulled me up and I found myself looking at a skinny kid with a round face.

"Hey dude, you okay?"

"I… I guess," I muttered. I glared at Blackboot, a big kid who glared back at me with dark eyes under a mop of greasy black hair as he slouched out of the room with a yellow detention slip clutched in his hand.

Chuck socked me on the shoulder. "Hey, forget him. You can sit by me. I'm Chuck."

"Ben."

I followed Chuck to the back of the room and slid into an empty desk. I kept my head low and wished that Chris and Fat Jimmy were here. They would pound that guy, for sure.

Dornegan The Dork

The bell rang. Chuck grabbed my schedule and gave it a once-over.

"Cool. We have math together. You'll like Mr. Fenton."

"No thanks." I grabbed my schedule and walked away. I wasn't in the market for new friends.

I looked back. Chuck stood there as if I told him his puppy just got run over. Whatever.

I don't care.

Blackboot showed up in the middle of math class. He stood in the doorway staring dead at me.

What is this dude's problem? I stared back. My grandpa always told me to never show your opponent fear, so I didn't.

The stare contest went on forever, until Mr. Fenton said, "Mr. Harry Dornegan. Take your seat now."

Harry Dornegan? What a dorky name, I thought. Dornegan the Dork.

I dragged my attention back to the teacher. Mr. Fenton couldn't stop blabbing about some ridiculous TV show called "Hello Singapore."

The TV host had supposedly posted a math riddle to his Facebook page asking kids to "guess Cheryl's birthday."

I raised my hand.

"Yes, Mr. Stark?"

"I don't get why you don't just Message them and say, "Hey Cheryl. When's your birthday?"

Some things, I just don't get about adults.

Mr. Fenton smiled. "Well, that would be cheating now, wouldn't it?"

I almost blurted out, "Who cares?" when the bell rang. I had just tossed my math book into my backpack when a big fist pounded on my desk.

"You got me in trouble."

"You got yourself in trouble."

"See ya at lunch, loser," Blackboot whispered, and bailed out the door.

"Not if I see you first!" I yelled, but he was gone.

Lunchtime Scraps

By the time I got to lunch, I was so hungry I was ready to chow down on my books.

I got a hamburger, potato chips, an apple, a banana, a carton of chocolate milk, and some cookies and headed toward an open seat.

"Hey Ben, over here." Chuck yelled. He slid his tray and scootched over to make room for me.

I pretended not to hear him. I was not in the mood to sit next to Mr. Goody Two Shoes and listen to him chatter about how great this place was. Besides, I have a reputation to keep, and nerd ain't it.

I plowed through the burnt hamburger and stale chips and moved on to the cookies when Blackboot slammed his tray next to mine, knocking my chocolate milk on the floor.

"Oops," he smirked. "Did I do that?"

That's it! This kid has gotten on my very last nerve.

Bam! My fist met Blackboot's nose.

Blood spurted.

Blackboot threw an arm around my neck and down we went in a ball of fury on the cafeteria floor.

The cafeteria went wild. "Fight, fight, fight!"

I squirmed out of Blackboot's grasp and landed another punch on his big fat nose, when a strong hand grabbed my neck and yanked me away.

"Come with me, Mr. Stark," the principal growled. "And you, Mr. Dornegan. Is this how we treat newcomers?"

"He started it!" yelled Blackboot.

"Shut-up, Dorky Dornegan!" I yelled back.

The crowd started screaming, "Dorky Dornegan! Dorky Dornegan!" until the vice principal, the gym coach, and Mr. Fenton ran in and started handing out detentions.

Mom is going to kill me, I thought. I can't even get through the first day without getting in trouble. I hate this place!

I crossed my arms and glared at Blackboot.

"Whatchoo lookin' at?" he grumbled.

"I might be the new kid," I snapped, "but I ain't gonna take any crap from you." I stared him right in the eye, the way my Pop-Pop taught me to stare down an enemy.

And that's when something surprising happened. Blackboot cracked a grin. "You sure can pack a punch," he said, touching his nose.

The door opened and Assistant Principal Waters stuck his head out. "Ben, I'll see you now."

I went in and he motioned me to take a seat in front of his desk. He strolled around his desk, sat, and paged through a thick file.

"I see from your records that you and your mom just moved here from Fort Hood, Texas?"

"Yes sir."

"I understand that moving can be difficult and especially having to begin at a new school." He paused like he was thinking. "However, we have a zero-tolerance policy for fighting. I've called your mother. She's on her way."

My heart thudded in my chest. They called my mom? I jumped to my feet. "It wasn't my fault," I protested. "That kid's a bully. He tripped me in class and then he knocked my tray on the floor at lunch…"

Mr. Waters held up one hand. "I need you to understand that your actions will not be tolerated. You are suspended for the rest of the week."

The phone buzzed. "Captain Stark is here, sir."

"Send her in."

My mom came in like a raging bull. Her lips were pressed together in a thin line, and her eyebrows were all squinched up like she was thinking up a million new ideas for punishing me. I could practically see the smoke coming out of her ears. I was seriously gonna get it.

I tried to show a look of surprise in an attempt to seek mercy from my mom while Mr. Waters filled her in. My mom sat next to me and listened to every word while I tried to shrink into a tiny little ball and disappear.

"I'll have his teachers make up homework packets for him to do at home," said Mr. Waters. "That way, he won't fall behind the other students."

My mom studied Mr. Waters. I knew that look. She had a plan.

"Ben, please wait for me in the other room," she said.

I grabbed my backpack and got outta there before she changed her mind.

In the car, I kept trying to tell Mom my side of the story, but she wouldn't listen. "Not now," was all she would say.

I thought maybe she wanted to wait until we got home, so we could have one of those deep talks she was always making me do.

But that didn't happen either. "Go to your room, Ben," was all she said when we got home, and then she went into her office and closed the door.

Not even a lecture.

I'm in trouble, big, deep-end-of-the-pool trouble, I thought as I trudged up the steps.

I slammed my door, kicked boxes out of my way, and fell on my bed. It was so unfair! Blackboot started it, and I'm the one in trouble.

A hot burning started in my throat, so I pulled a pillow over my head. I didn't want Mom to hear me crying.

From Bad to Worse

I woke to the sound of my mom calling me down for dinner. Dang. I didn't even remember falling asleep.

The smell of garlic spaghetti sauce pulled me downstairs like a magnet.

"Have a seat, sleepyhead," said Mom, setting a big bowl of spaghetti with extra-large meatballs and a plate of cheesy garlic bread on the table. Yum! My favorite.

Mom took a two-liter bottle out of the fridge. "Soda?"

"Really?"

"Really." Mom filled my glass and spooned a pile of spaghetti and meatballs on my plate. I dug in like I hadn't eaten all day. It seemed like forever since the burnt hamburger and stale chips.

For a few minutes, things felt so normal. Mom and me, in our clean kitchen, eating yummy food, music playing in the background. My tummy filled and I relaxed. No matter how much we moved, I always had my mom and her cooking.

Mom leaned back and sipped her soda. "We have to talk about today."

And just like that, the warm feeling in my tummy turned to a barfy one. "I know I got suspended, but…"

"No, you didn't. You're going to school tomorrow."

Wait. What?

"What?"

"Let's just say reason prevailed." Mom chased a meatball around with her fork.

"Sooo… does that mean I'm not in trouble?"

"Listen Ben. I know this move has been tough on you, but your behavior at school today is not okay."

"But he started it…"

"I don't care who started it. I've taught you better than that."

I stared at the half-piece of bread on my plate. "Yes ma'am," I mumbled. "So, what's my punishment?"

Mom sighed. "No punishment."

"Really?"

"It's your first day, and I know how much you miss Chris and Fat Jimmy," she said. "You're a good boy, Ben, and I love you very much."

I flung myself out of my chair and hugged my mom tight. "Thanks, Mom," I whispered. "I won't let you down again."

"I know."

I happily cleared the plates off the table and put them in the sink.

"I picked up some ice cream. Get it out, will you?"

I opened the freezer. Peanut butter fudge. My all-time favorite.

I scooped out ice cream while my mom loaded the dishwasher. We sat down again, and then she said it.

"Ben. I have something to tell you."

Oh crap.

"Don't tell me we're moving again already," I joked, but she didn't even crack a grin.

Mom took a deep breath as she looked me straight in my eyes……for a really weird long time. "What I am going to tell you is very difficult."

Now she had my full attention. I pushed away my ice cream. "Just tell me already."

Mom sighed again, and this time, I thought I saw tears in her eyes.

"Well, my unit has been asked to go and help our friends in another country because some of their unfriendly neighbors are bullying them."

"So you're going there to stop it?"

"Yes."

"Are you going to teach them how to fight back?"

"Maybe. It's hard to say until we get there."

I tapped my fingers on the table. "When I got bullied today, you said I'm not allowed to fight back."

Mom gasped a tiny bit, and her eyes got big. "That's not exactly the same thing."

"You said they're getting bullied. I got bullied too."

"Ben, sometimes being in the Army means that we have to leave home and take care of other people who might not be as fortunate as we are."

"As a nurse, it is my job to help take care of Soldiers and our friends that are sick, even if that means going to a place that is far away from home."

"That's not fair!" I jumped up and paced around the kitchen.

Mom's sad eyes were glued on me. "I know."

"This sucks!"

"It does."

"Is this why you fixed my favorite meal? To trick me?" How could she do this to me?

Mom sat quietly as I stomped around, but then I saw real tears streaming down her cheeks, and I stopped dead in my tracks.

Mom saw me seeing. She wiped her face, then slammed the ice cream dishes in the sink and stood there with her back to me, taking in deep breaths. She only does this when she is trying to calm down. I wasn't sure if I should go to her, or if she needed a minute, so I just stood there.

Mom turned and placed her hands on my face. Her eyes were red and puffy, and tears streamed down her face.

"Ben," Mom said, "I love you. I would never lie to you. You and I are a team, and nothing will ever change that. You are the most important person on earth and your happiness is more important to me than anything else in the world."

I usually loved how her soft hands felt on my face. She would always touch my face when I was upset, and her touch was like a cool cloth.

"But Mom," I asked, "What if you die?"

Worry lines etched into her forehead. Mom dropped her head and for the first time, she had no words.

I got up from the table, knocking the chair backwards onto the floor, and ran to my room.

That Most Horrible Night

My head was spinning, racing with all sorts of Blood and Guts Military Movie thoughts. I told myself to stop, took a moment to breathe, and tried to take my mind off my mom's awful news by dumping boxes littering my floor. I tossed clothes into drawers, shoes into my closet, and stuffed last year's stash of Halloween candy into my backpack. I stacked books on my bookcase, although not in any order.

I dumped another box, and something jangly fell on the floor. I picked up my dad's dog tags and held them in my hands. Where did these come from? I didn't remember packing them in this box, but here they were. It was like my dad was there, saying hi. My hands shook, but I slipped them over my head and under my shirt.

I thought about my dad. When he was alive, Dad would lift me in the air with his strong arms and toss me, singing, "Look at Ben-Ben flying so high, look at Ben-Ben soaring through the sky."

My dad was my hero.

It wasn't too long after I turned five that my father died. Although I was only five when he died, I still remember lots of things about him.

Some of my favorite memories was when he would wrestle with me and tickle me till my face was sore from laughing.

Dad would also take me to the park and let me run around with the other kids until I was so tired that I'd fall asleep while he carried me to the car.

I miss how my dad would move through our house. His feet clunked heavy in his military boots. I could hear the loud thump of his feet as he walked across our wooden floors that creaked right before he entered the bathroom. This was dad's routine each morning as he prepared for work.

I dumped the last box and stacked some games on my bookcase.

The last thing I remember about my dad was when he put on his uniform and kissed Mom and me on the forehead as he always did and left for work. This was the day my dad never returned home. I remember Mom calling everyone she knew to see if they knew where Dad was.

I laid on my bed and thought about what happened later that night, that horrible night. My mom answered the door and saw two men in their fancy military uniforms. The soldiers told my mom that Dad was in a training accident and he was not coming home.

Ever.

I could feel my mom's legs tremble as she fell onto the ground. I did not know what was going on then, and I remember being really scared. When I saw my mom on the floor, crying, I got really scared and bawled my head off.

When I got older, my mom explained to me that dad was driving a vehicle and it rolled over and fell into an 18-foot ravine.

The memory brought burning tears up. I turned on my TV to distract myself, but it wasn't hooked up yet. Dang it!

I tried to read a book, but I couldn't stop thinking about that most horrible night. My thoughts keep racing back to how my mom was getting deployed and how those guys in fancy uniforms were going to show up here telling me my mom wasn't coming back home. Ugh! I hate this life.

L.T. Hutchinson

Skipping School

I woke up with the worst headache ever. Eyes bloodshot and puffy like I was in a fight and I did not win.

I gave myself a moment to shake the sleep off my brain before I jumped out of bed, got dressed, and whipped out of the house. I didn't want my mom taking me to school and making me "talk about it" anymore.

I found the bus stop and took my place near the end of the line. Being in the back of the line meant I would get a seat in the back of the bus. This was my favorite place because it's the farthest away from those pesky kindergarteners and those girls who chatter non-stop.

My thoughts drift to my best friends Chris and Fat Jimmy. We always sat in the back of the bus. Fat Jimmy is this tall, skinny kid who can tell you all the stats for any major league basketball player. I still scratch my head at how Fat Jimmy was able to hold all of those facts in his head yet couldn't pass math class to save his life.

Then there's Chris. Chris is short and built like a tank and loves basketball more than his mother. He carries his basketball, signed by Michael Jordan, around with him everywhere. Sometimes, when Chris and Fat Jimmy talk basketball, it's like they're speaking Spanish, or French, or maybe Martian.

Come to think of it, not sure why we call him Fat Jimmy, but it just stuck when we learned that he was able to keep all those facts in his fat brain.

When I landed at that school in Ft. Bragg, those guys pulled me into a game of HORSE. They totally creamed me, but I didn't care. They were cool and didn't even care that I was the new kid. I was just one of the guys, just like that.

I sighed. I was happy there. My mom's job was easy for her, and she was home every day when I got home from school. I even had a basketball hoop in the driveway.

But here, it's different and weird. My friends are back at my old school, my dad is gone, and now my mom is getting sent to a bad place. And worst of all, this school was full of bullies.

The school bus stopped with a jolt. The brakes let out a sound that reminded me of an old freight train whistling out steam as it cruised into the station. The door slammed open and the driver gave us a "get out of here" wave without even looking at us.

I began to follow the herd, but then my feet turned me around and connected with my legs and my arms as I jolted in a full stride toward the football field.

I camped out under the bleachers. It was nice here – quiet, with no eyes looking at me. I dug the candy out of my backpack and munched while I played my Nintendo Switch. Maybe I could just live here.

The bleachers clanked as Dornegan the Dork's black boots stomped over my head and he spotted me in my hiding place. "Dude! Is that a Switch?" he said.

Dorkey Dornegan

Blackboot jumped down, plopped next to me, grabbed my Switch from my hand, and started playing.

"Why you here, Mr. New Kid?" he said. "Ain't your type supposed to be in class sucking up to the teachers?"

"Everyone there is stupid," I mumbled.

Blackboot stopped playing, stared at me, and laughed out loud. "Got that right. Maybe you ain't so bad," he said, and clobbered me on the shoulder.

Blackboot bent over my Switch and what do you know – a set of dog tags fell out from under his shirt. The dog tags had lots of keys attached.

Then it got weird.

Blackboot looked all scared and shoved the dog tags back under his shirt. He shot me a look like "did you see?" and went back to playing the game.

Why would he want to hide those?

"Those your dad's?" I asked.

"What?"

"Those dog tags."

"Why do you care?" said Blackboot.

"I got my dad's, too," I said, and pulled them out.

That got his attention.

"Really? Those are your dad's? Why isn't he wearing them?"

"Why do you care?" I mimicked him.

And then things got really weird.

Blackboot took out his dog tags. "My dad died in Afghanistan," he said simply, "and this is all I got left."

Blackboot quickly put his dad's dog tags back under his shirt and walked away with his hands stuffed in his pockets.

"Wait!" I jogged after him. "My dad died too, in a training accident."

"No kidding?"

"For reals."

He held out one hand. "Can I see?"

I handed over my dad's dog tags, and he handed his to me. I read them carefully and handed them back. It was weird. It felt like something had changed, like now we were in some kind of secret club or something.

We spent the rest of the day playing Super Smash and eating stale Halloween candy. Just like friends.

Pop-Pop and Gran-Fan

The next couple weeks went by too fast as Mom got ready to deploy. Even with all that, I watched her while she tried really hard to get all the boxes unpacked and get the house what she called "a place of comfort and refuge." I liked it because I finally got TV and Internet and could Skype and email with Chris and Fat Jimmy. Things seemed normal, so I just made myself forget about her leaving.

"C'mon, Ben," she said one day. "We're going to hit the PX and the commissary."

"Do I have to?" I grumped at her. "I just got online with Chris and Fat Jimmy to play Smash."

She shot me The Look. "Gran-Fan gave me a list. I need your help to stock up today because they're arriving tomorrow. So get moving, mister."

I felt like she had punched me in the gut. Tomorrow? Already?

Mom had made arrangements for my grandparents Gran-Fan and Pop-Pop to move in here with us. She said I had to stay in my school and keep things as normal as possible… yeah, like anything is ever normal in the Army.

Don't get me wrong. I was super hyped that they were coming. Gran-Fan makes these cakes that melt in your mouth, and Pop-Pop was cool, like a buddy... only with gray hair.

I signed off and dragged my feet to the car. If my grandparents were coming, that meant Mom was leaving soon.

I guess I did my forgetting too well.

After we unloaded the car and put away all the groceries, we made up the guest room all nice and cozy.

"Now can I go play Smash?" I said.

Mom smiled at me. "Go get the special presents, and then yes, you can play."

I grabbed two brightly-wrapped gifts and set them on the dresser in the guest room. I turned, ready for Smash, but my mom was sitting on the edge of the bed, staring at me.

I caught her eye, and she stood up. "Thanks, buddy."

"Mom."

"Hmm?"

I threw my arms around her and hugged her tighter than I ever did before. Her body trembled, and her tears fell on my neck.

"I'm keeping you home today," Mom announced over a breakfast of French toast.

I stopped shoveling the cinnamon-y French toast into my mouth. Did I hear her right?

"Really?"

"Yep. Your grandparents will be here around lunchtime. I know you want to see them and they can't wait to see you."

"Cool!"

They actually got there early (big surprise – Pop-Pop says if you're on time, you're late). I ran out to meet them, and their big, slobbery Golden Retriever, Sarge.

Gran-Fan immediately wrapped her large soft, inviting arms around my body. Her hugs were like being wrapped in a warm blanket. Waves of comfort washed right to the tip of my toes. Like a baby, I gave in to her warmth and sank into her arms like a marshmallow melting on the end of a heated stick.

Pop-Pop waited patiently for his handshake. He never hugs because he says that's not what men do when they greet each other.

I stood straight up and firmly gripped Pop-Pop's hands, giving him the strongest shake, I could muster, and he instantly fell to his knees. "Ow, boy, let go!" We both laughed and did this fist-and-elbow bumping thing we invented.

Pop-Pop was wearing his favorite fishing cap and a bright red flannel shirt with a vest that has way too many pockets. No joke, each pocket was filled to the brim with all sorts of fishing thingies and of course his favorite caramel candy that he sneaked when Gran-Fan wasn't looking.

Pop-Pop took two fishing rods and a tacklebox out of his car and grinned. "Fishing trip this weekend, buddy."

I jumped at least five feet off the ground. "Yes!"

"Not only are we going fishing," said Pop-Pop, "but we are also going camping for three magnificent man-filled days. So, get packed and let's skedaddle."

The Great Camping Trip

Pop-Pop stuck a marshmallow on a stick, and I held it over the open fire. The sky was bright, the sun felt warm, and frogs croaked lazily in the reeds. Sarge was romping around, chasing squirrels up trees, and barking happily.

"Pop-Pop?" I asked.

"Hm?"

"Who made up s'mores?"

Pop-Pop laughed so hard he didn't see his marshmallow melt off the stick and plop into the fire. "Dunno," he said. "What do you think?"

"I think it was accidental, you know, like maybe some kids were camping, and one had some chocolate, and one had some marshmallows…"

"And one thought about squishing them into a graham cracker?"

"Maybe."

Pop-Pop got that thinking look on his face. "That's a good story," he said. "Let's go with it."

I yawned big. "I'm stuffed. Can we just pitch our tents and chill for the rest of the day?"

"I did not come all the way to these God-graced woods to lay up in a tent with you all day and smell your farts. We are going fishing."

I grabbed my rod and tacklebox and followed Pop-Pop on the short walk to the pond. The water was still, with only a few ripples shimmering across the surface.

I grabbed a slimy worm from the Styrofoam cup filled with dirt we purchased from a roadside store on the way in. I cast my rod into the pond and waited for some innocent fish to decide it wanted lunch.

Our fish count for the year more than doubled during our camping trip, from two to four. It was my job to clean them and Pop-Pop cooked them up.

"That fish sure smells good," I said. Pop-Pop cooked blue catfish on the fire that lit up our entire campsite while I lay on my back and counted stars with Sarge beside me.

"Knock! Knock."

Who's there?" I rolled my eyes. Pop-Pop loves his jokes.

"Impatient cow."

"Impatient cow who?"

"Impatient Cow MOO!"

"Ha-Ha. Not very funny, Pop-Pop." But I grinned anyway at the look on his face.

We ate more catfish and beans, and watched the moon rise high in the sky.

"Pop-Pop?"

"Hmm?"

"Why is the Army sending Mom away?"

Pop-Pop was quiet for a long time. Then he sighed, an intense, long sigh that came from deep inside him. "It's a shame, them sending your mom away."

"I don't want her to go."

"Nor do I. Or your Gran-Fan. Or your mom."

"You don't think Mom wants to go?"

Pop-Pop scraped the dinner plates clean and tucked them away. "No, son. She does not. Want some water?"

"Yes, please."

I thought about this while Pop-Pop got out a couple water bottles from his favorite green cooler and handed one to me.

"Pop-Pop?"

"I'm listening."

"What if…" My lip trembled and my throat clutched up. "What if she doesn't come back?"

Pop-Pop tossed a log on the fire, sending sparks flying into the night. "Well, son, guess you can't live your life worrying about all the things that could happen."

"But, my dad got killed and he was just doing his job in the Army."

Pop-Pop sighed again. "Damn shame."

"And Mom is going to a place where bad things happen all the time…"

Pop-Pop stretched out his legs. "I don't have the answers, son, but one thing I do know."

"What?"

"Your mom loves you more than anything else in this world. So, no matter what happens, you can count on that."

I thought about that for a long time, even after my Pop-Pop's gentle snores rumbled in the night.

Early the next day, we packed up our gear, made sure our campsite was cleaner than how we found it, and headed back home. Smokey the Bear would be proud of us.

Our drive home was quiet as we traveled through the curvy mountainous hills of North Carolina's Great Smokey Mountains. Somewhere along those curves, I fell asleep and didn't wake up until Pop-Pop was pulling up in our driveway.

Roundtop Mountain

Mom and Gran-Fan loved hearing about our magnificent, man-filled adventures.

"…and I caught four of the largest blue catfish ever recorded in history, and…"

A hard knock on the door interrupted my fish tale. I looked through the picture window and saw Blackboot slouching there.

"Hey," I said, opening the door.

"Hey. Want to come hang with me? I can show you some cool stuff."

"Sure."

I grabbed my bike and followed Blackboot as he sped through our neighborhood like a pro. I huffed and puffed to keep up with his pace.

We attacked the biggest and baddest dirt mountain I ever saw, speeding around curvy hills and steep cliffs that went on forever.

We finally stopped at the top of the mountain and plopped under the shade of some trees to rest.

"What's this place?" I asked.

Blackboot handed me a bottle of water and a granola bar from his backpack. "Roundtop Mountain. This is where the Soldiers parachute out of planes for practice."

"It's a pretty cool place to chill."

"Yeah," Blackboot said. "This spot here is my fave. Wanna see something?"

"Sure."

Blackboot dug in the dirt near a rock and moved some twigs and came up with an old tin box.

"This is where I stash stuff I collect," Blackboot said. He pulled off his dad's dog tags and placed them in the tin box.

"Why are you doing that?" I asked. "Don't you want to keep them?"

Blackboot stuffed the tin box back in the hole and covered it up. "It's safer here."

"Safer?"

Blackboot shrugged. "My fake father is a jerk."

"What's a fake father?"

"He's a step. My mom married him a year ago, and now we're stuck here."

I nodded. "Let me guess. The Army decides your life."

"Pretty much."

I took a bite of granola bar because I didn't really know what to say. "I'm sorry about your dad."

"Yeah. Me too."

I finished my snack and stood up. "What's over there?"

"This is the Sidewinder bike path," Blackboot stood and we walked to the edge of a steep cliff. "Kids used to come here to practically fly down that steep part there. See?"

I looked where he pointed. It looked like it went straight down.

"Did you do it?" I asked.

"Heck no. A kid got killed there."

"What?"

I peeked over and my heart started pounding. Trees stuck out from the mountain like spikes and the drop looked like it was a gazillion feet down.

I backed away from the edge.

"So what happened to that kid?"

"Liam dropped down here…" Blackboot pointed at a spot that looked like it could be a path, "and made it about halfway. But then he hit a tree root and pitched over the edge."

I stared at Blackboot. "Liam? You knew him?"

Blackboot stared at his black boots. "He was my brother." And then he grabbed his bike and zoomed away.

I followed behind him, thinking hard.

Deployment Day

Pop-Pop, Gran-Fan, and I took Mom to Pope Air Force Base on Fort Bragg. The ride took forever. I had nightmares the whole night before. The worst one was my mom flying off a cliff on a mountain bike, and falling and screaming…

"Ben, wake up." Mom shook my shoulder. I'd fallen asleep with my head against the window.

"Sorry," I mumbled, and then I just blurted out the thing that was bothering me. "What if you, I mean, what if something bad happens?"

"Oh sweetheart. I promise, I will stay safe, and I will come home to you. And we will Skype. Every day."

"Okay."

We finally got a parking space. I couldn't believe how many people were there. Whole families came to say goodbye to their soldier. Some were kids younger than me.

The Army tried to cheer us up by bringing a band made up of other Soldiers to play music. How stupid was that? Like this was a party? Like that made it okay to send my mom to a place with bombs and guns and people trying to kill her. Yeah. Great.

"Time to say our goodbyes now," said Pop-Pop.

Hugging my mom was kind of hard because she had a large green camouflaged backpack filled with all her stuff for the long flight. But then she dropped it on the ground, wrapped her arms tight around me, and hugged me harder than she ever had before.

"Remember Ben. We are a team and I will be with you right here all the time," she said, making the shape of a heart with her hand and holding it over her heart.

I made the same shape, placed it over my heart, and hugged her hard.

I stood between Pop-Pop and Gran-Fan and watched my mom trudge up the ramp into the back of the plane. I waited for her to turn and wave, but she didn't. Gran-Fan thinks she was trying not to cry.

The New Normal

Days turned into months, and Mom was still gone. School sucks. Everyone is always yelling at me to do my homework.

Why bother, it is so stupid and pointless. Why should I? I probably won't even be at this school next year anyway.

At least today is Friday. I ran home, threw my backpack on the floor in my room, and got my iPad. Time to Skype with my mom.

My iPad rang. "Hi Mom!"

"Hi Ben. How are you?"

"Good. Pop-Pop is taking me to the carnival tomorrow."

Mom laughed. "Uh-oh. They better oil up the roller coaster."

We laughed. Pop-Pop and I once rode the roller coaster in Belmont Park in San Diego twenty times in a row.

"How's school?"

"Fine." That was a lie. "I got an A on my spelling test." At least that was true. Spelling was easy.

"Wonderful! And how are Pop-Pop and Gran-Fan?"

"Gran-Fan is making a special surprise for supper – I think its chocolate cheesecake - and Pop-Pop is doing yoga on the front lawn with Sarge. He says he has to stretch his back so he can keep up with me at the carnival. When are you coming home?"

"Are you keeping up with the calendar we made?"

"Yeah." Mom got a special calendar so I could mark off the days. "It says you've been gone for six months."

"That's a long time. But it also means we're over the hump, right? Now we can start counting down."

"Yeah." I wanted her to say she was coming home, but she didn't, so I just kept my mouth shut. Gran-Fan said I shouldn't stress out my mom.

We talked for a while longer, and then Mom said she had to get off.

"Same time tomorrow?" I asked her.

Mom made the shape of a heart and placed it over her heart, and I did the same and we both said together "We are a team."

We hung up and I followed my nose into the kitchen. "What's for supper?"

"I made my famous, sure to put you in a good mood, fried chicken, collards, and red beans and rice."

"And chocolate cheesecake for dessert?"

"You got it."

"That's one of my favorite meals!"

"I know," she smiled. "Set the table and then call your Pop-Pop. Let's eat."

Carnival!

I got up on Saturday ready for carnival fun. I found Gran-Fan and Pop-Pop huddled at the kitchen table, sharing the morning paper, and drinking coffee from their favorite coffee mugs. Pop-Pop's mug had a picture of Sarge on it. Gran-Fan's mug had a garden of flowers and butterflies.

"Good morning, sleepyhead," said Gran-Fan. "Help yourself to cereal. There's orange juice too, and biscuits."

I poured a giant bowl of Capt. Crunch, then drowned my biscuit in butter and honey. Mm, Gran-Fan's biscuits. My favorite.

"Why do you have the T.V blasting so loud?" I asked Pop-Pop.

"Need to know if I should pack a bug-out bag to run from the zombies, or an umbrella for the rain."

"Can you just put on the words?" I said. "It hurts my ears."

Pop-Pop grumbled but did as I asked.

I finished my cereal, and we were almost out the door when the phone rang.

"Hello?" Gran-Fan said. There was a pause, and then she dropped the phone.

"Helen!" Pop-Pop ran to her. She looked like someone had punched her in the gut. Pop-Pop helped her to a chair, picked up the phone, and barked, "Who is this?"

There was a long pause. Pop-Pop reached out and pulled a chair over to sit down.

"I understand," he said finally, and hung up.

My stomach flip-flopped. Something bad happened. I could tell. I didn't like the way they were looking at me.

"Are we going now?" I asked. My voice came out sounding like a mouse squeak.

Pop-Pop looked at Gran-Fan and she shrugged.

"Sure," he said, smiling big. "But first, sit down."

I perched on the edge of a chair.

"Looks like your mom is coming home early, son," said Pop-Pop.

"What? Yes!" I jumped up and punched the air.

Pop-Pop and Gran-Fan looked at each other. Gran-Fan looked like she wanted to say something, but Pop-Pop put a hand on her shoulder.

"Ready to go have our carnival day?" he asked.

I grinned from ear to ear. "Bet I can ride the Ferris Wheel more times than you." And off we went, leaving Gran-Fan and Sarge to do the dishes.

I didn't know that would be the last fun day for a long time.

The Return

Three weeks later, we stood at International arrivals. I kept looking for my mom, but all these people passed, and no mom.

"Where is she?" I complained.

"She's there," said Pop-Pop in this weird voice. I looked where he pointed, but it was just someone in a wheelchair, all bruised up and hunched over, with a big ole cast on her leg and a lot of bandages around her head.

"That's not her."

But Pop-Pop and Gran-Fan went to the wheelchair lady and hugged her. "You're home," Pop-Pop said.

"Where's Ben?" Mom mumbled. She stared at me and held out a hand. "Is that you?" She sounded funny, like her mouth was filled with cotton balls.

I just stared at her. I was afraid to hug her. What if I hurt her more?

"Let's go home," said Gran-Fan. "I made pizza." She sounded chirpy, like a bird. I don't like her chirpy bird voice. That's when I knew this was way worse than I thought.

While Gran-Fan tucked Mom into bed, Pop-Pop went into the kitchen to yell at someone on the phone. I sat on the floor outside the kitchen and listened cuz I wanted to know what's wrong with my mom, too.

"You tell me right now what is wrong with my daughter," Pop-Pop growled in that don't-mess-with-me Colonel's voice he once used when he was in the Army and was mad.

There was a long pause and then he said, "A Traumatic Brain Injury?"

There was a thunk as Pop-Pop dropped the phone. I peeked in. He had his face in his hands and his shoulders were moving like he was crying.

That's when I knew Mom's return was worse than worse.

Mom Isn't Mom

The shock of my mom's injuries hurt my grandparents a lot.

Pop-Pop would stay on the couch, staring at the television. I could hear him in the middle of the night and in the morning, I would see him still on the couch in the same spot.

Gran-Fan was always in the kitchen, baking non-stop. I didn't even know that coconut cupcakes were a thing. And when she wasn't baking, she spent hours in my mom's bedroom, reading to her (which she liked) and trying to get her to do yoga stretches (which made Mom throw things).

My house used to be a place where I felt safe, even when we had to move. Now it felt like a war zone. Even normal things sometimes made my mom scream and throw things. This morning, Mom was in the kitchen in her wheelchair. Gran-Fan started to pour her a cup of coffee, and Mom said she could do it herself. But her hands shook, and she dropped the pot on the floor, splashing all of us with hot coffee and breaking the carafe into a million pieces.

I didn't know what a traumatic brain injury was, but I know it made my mom different.

She sometimes couldn't remember my name, she was always angry, and she didn't even know how to drink freaking coffee! What the heck?

I couldn't stand it. I bailed and aimed my bike up to Roundtop mountain. All I could think was *she promised me that she wasn't going to get hurt but she lied.*

I found a nice shady spot and sat on the edge with my feet dangling over, wondering what it would feel like to just slip off the edge. Would it hurt to fall that far? Would anyone even notice if I didn't go back? Would it matter?

I cried for a long time.

Mr. Fenton

I went to school, but just put my head down on my desk and waited for the bell to ring.

"Mr. Stark!" Mr. Fenton yelled my name. He looked really irritated.

"What?"

"Please see me after class."

"Whatever."

Great. Just great.

I stayed in my seat when the bell rang. I was probably gonna get suspended for this, but so what? It didn't matter anyway.

Mr. Fenton sat across from me and took a deep breath. "I heard about your mom, Ben. I'm really sorry."

I sat up and stared at him. Was he making fun of me?

But Mr. Fenton just looked sorry.

"Yeah. Whatever. Can I go?"

"Not yet." Another deep breath. "When I was just a little older than you, my parents both got deployed at the same time."

Wait… what?

"It was horrible," Mr. Fenton continued. "I had to go to stay with my uncle in Chicago. He liked to drink, scotch I think, and he had a different girl… well, never mind. Let's just say I was lucky if he remembered to buy food, much less give a crap if I was there or not."

"What did you do?"

He slung one arm on the table. "Well, mostly I cut school. I used to skateboard along Lake Michigan, even when it snowed. Anything was better than being at home."

"Did your parents come home?"

A sad smile flitted across his face. "My mom did," he said, "but my dad…no. So I get it."

I stared at him. Seriously?

"Can I go now?"

Mr. Fenton gave me a long look. "Yes. I'll write you a pass."

I snatched it away and ran out the door.

No Show

I opened my front door to chaos.

"NO NO NO! I can do it myself." Mom picked up a fork and tried to scoop her soup. Gran-Fan gently tried to switch the spoon for the fork, but Mom slapped her hand away.

"NO!"

I watched my calm, level-headed mother turn into a screeching banshee. She threw the fork and slammed her fists on the table and burst into tears. Sarge scurried out of the room when the fork bonked him on the head.

Moving slowly, Pop-Pop gently slipped a spoon into her hand. "Try again, baby."

Mom scooped up some soup and managed to get it into her mouth. "See Daddy? I told you I could do this." And just like that, Mom turned as docile as a bunny.

"Hey Mom," I said. "How are you?"

"Hi, Benny," she said and sipped more soup. *Benny?*

"Hey grandson!" Pop-Pop boomed. "You're home early."

"Yeah, I, um, they let us out early," I stuttered, not looking at Pop-Pop.

"Half-day, honey?" asked Gran-Fan. She took a cherry pie out of the oven and set it on the counter to cool. "We often had those when I was teaching. Gives the teachers time to catch up."

"Right," I said. My stomach churned, and I made a beeline out of the kitchen and up to my room.

"Ben. We need to talk." Pop-Pop came into my room and leaned against the wall. He ran his hand through his hair, and suddenly, I realized that he looked tired. And old.

Wrinkles I had never noticed before lined his eyes and mouth. His hair looked thin and gray.

"What's up Pop-Pop?"

"I know school didn't let out early."

"Ugh…how do you know that?"

"Funny thing. When you failed to make it to your last period class, the principal called to let me know you were a no-show."

"So what? I didn't go to English. No big deal. Mom doesn't care. She doesn't even know."

Pop-Pop sighed heavily and sat on the edge of the bed. "I don't know what to tell you, son. Your momma's head was hit hard. She has a traumatic brain injury. When that happens, things don't always go back to normal right away. You just have to give her time."

"I'm tired of giving it time."

"I'm sorry you have to go through this, son, but we have to pull together as a family. You know that."

I pulled a pillow over my head. "Maybe I just won't be in this family anymore."

Pop-Pop sighed again and stood up. "Listen up, boy. I can't keep putting up with your attitude and take care of your momma, too. You better shape up. No more cutting school, you hear?"

My door slammed.

I had never heard my Pop-Pop sound so mad.

No More

I grabbed my bike and raced away from my home as fast as my bike could take me. I just wanted to get away and go anywhere but school or home. I raced past kids playing in the park with their parents. I looked at them and instantly hated them for having both of their parents. They looked HAPPY…they looked normal.

I aimed my bike towards Roundtop Mountain and stood on the pedals as I pumped. "Why is this happening to me?" I yelled out loud. I didn't really expect an answer, but I liked yelling at the sky. The sky was clear, and puffy marshmallow clouds floated there. This almost seemed like a normal day if you weren't me.

I kept going, huffing and puffing and wondering why I didn't know how to be happy anymore. I want my mom to be herself again. I want to go back to Ft. Hood. I want my dad to be alive and for him and Mom to be together again, like it was when I was five. I felt my dad's dog tags bouncing against my chest… and then I let him have it.

"Where were you? You left me and Mom alone. Why? Now Mom is sick with some stupid brain thing and she can't even remember who I am most of the time."

My bike wheels clicked on the chain that Fat Jimmy helped me rig with a playing card. I got to the top and kept going, aiming for the steep path where Liam had died.

Dirt made a small cloud around my feet as I picked up speed. I wasn't scared, I wasn't afraid anymore. I want the hurt to stop. I was tired of the pep talks, pats on the back, and the looks I get from teachers when I mess up again and again. And I was exhausted from being at home with Mom's tantrums and screaming and the sad faces on Gran-Fan and Pop-Pop.

Wind blew in my face as I got close to the edge. For a split second, my feet went backwards on the pedal to put on the brakes, and I thought I heard Dornegan yelling, "Stop! Ben, stop!"

It was too late. My bike tipped over the cliff.

The Last Chapter. Maybe

This is a very special book, because, as you can see, it does not have an ending like a regular book.

What what?

No, I didn't forget to write the ending. I have a plan and that plan is that you are going to help me by being the author. That's right! You are now an author, just like me.

Now it's your job to write the ending of this book. You can write any ending you want. It could be sad, or funny, or happy, or anything else you wish. This book is now your story.

Here are some tips to help you get started. Ask yourself:

What do you think happens to Ben?

What happens to Ben's mom?

What do you think happens to Dorky Dornegan?

Is Chuck going to become friends with Ben?

Could Ben ask Mr. Fenton for help?

Remember, you don't have to worry about spelling, punctuation, or grammar. Just do your best.

What is way more important is what happens in the story. And that's where you get to use your imagination and be creative.

So go on and write your story! And have some fun with it.

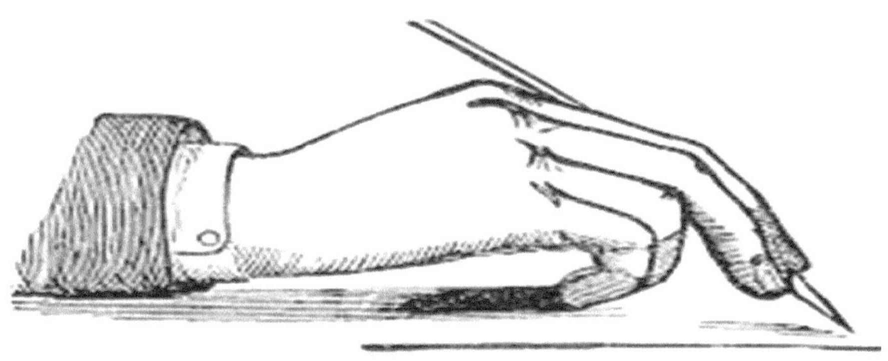

Acknowledgments

I would like to thank all the people who helped me bring this book into the world. My deepest gratitude to:

My family for your loving support in all things…

My mentor Neno Easter. For your guidance, coaching, and mentorship since I was a Major in the United States Army. You've helped nourish my career throughout the years, and I appreciate all the time you've dedicated to me and so many other Soldiers.

My Army brother Steve Opet. We served together while on Active Duty for a few years and have traveled many miles together. Even though it has been a few years since we last spoke, you never wavered when I called and asked for assistance in illustrating my book. Thank you for all your support.

My Army brother James Billings. I can't say enough how you and your family have blessed me throughout the years. Your family embraced me early on and to this day you've never let go. Thank you for editing and reviewing my book and more importantly, being a light during one of the darkest moments in my life.